CELEBRATING THE FAMILY NAME OF WAGNER

Celebrating the Family Name of Wagner

Walter the Educator

Silent King Books
a WhichHead Entertainment Imprint

Copyright © 2024 by Walter the Educator

All rights reserved. No part of this book may be reproduced in any manner whatsoever without written permission except in the case of brief quotations embodied in critical articles and reviews.

First Printing, 2024

Disclaimer

This book is a literary work; the story is not about specific persons, locations, situations, and/or circumstances unless mentioned in a historical context. Any resemblance to real persons, locations, situations, and/or circumstances is coincidental. This book is for entertainment and informational purposes only. The author and publisher offer this information without warranties expressed or implied. No matter the grounds, neither the author nor the publisher will be accountable for any losses, injuries, or other damages caused by the reader's use of this book. The use of this book acknowledges an understanding and acceptance of this disclaimer.

Celebrating the Family Name of Wagner is a memory book that belongs to the Celebrating Family Name Book Series by Walter the Educator. Collect them all and more books at WaltertheEducator.com

USE THE EXTRA SPACE TO DOCUMENT YOUR FAMILY MEMORIES THROUGHOUT THE YEARS

WAGNER

The name of Wagner, bold and bright,

Celebrating the Family Name of

Wagner

A banner lifted into light,

Through ages past and days to come,

A legacy that will not numb.

In lands where mountains touch the sky,

Where rivers deep in shadows lie,

The Wagners built their dreams from stone,

With hearts of fire and hands of bone.

Through trials fierce and triumphs sweet,

They walked their path with steady feet.

Each generation carved its way,

With strength that time cannot decay.

The Wagner name, a song unsung,

But in its heart, an anthem rung

Of those who labored, those who fought,

Of lives with love and purpose wrought.

Celebrating the Family Name of

Wagner

In fields of gold or winter's chill,

Their spirits bent but never still.

Through battles won and battles lost,

They understood that life had cost.

And still, they rose with heads held high,

Their vision locked upon the sky.

A family bound by honor's thread,

By stories told and prayers said.

The Wagners walk through storm and sun,

United as though forged as one.

In every hand, a strength is found,

That ties them to the fertile ground.

From forests dense to cities wide,

Their roots run deep, their reach is wide.

Celebrating the Family Name of

Wagner

The name they bear, it calls to all,

To rise again, to never fall.

The Wagner blood, it flows with pride,

In every soul, a flame inside.

For those who passed, for those to come,

Their voices form a steady hum.

In art and craft, in trade and toil,

Their legacy lives in the soil.

For every step they dared to take,

The world has shifted in their wake.

ABOUT THE CREATOR

Walter the Educator is one of the pseudonyms for Walter Anderson. Formally educated in Chemistry, Business, and Education, he is an educator, an author, a diverse entrepreneur, and he is the son of a disabled war veteran. "Walter the Educator" shares his time between educating and creating. He holds interests and owns several creative projects that entertain, enlighten, enhance, and educate, hoping to inspire and motivate you. Follow, find new works, and stay up to date with Walter the Educator™ at WaltertheEducator.com

www.ingramcontent.com/pod-product-compliance
Lightning Source LLC
LaVergne TN
LVHW052009060526
838201LV00059B/3926